ARACHNID WORLD
CRAB SPIDERS

SANDRA MARKLE

PHANTOM HUNTERS

◢ LERNER PUBLICATIONS COMPANY MINNEAPOLIS

FOR CURIOUS KIDS EVERYWHERE

ACKNOWLEDGMENTS

The author would like to thank Dr. Gary Dodson, Ball State University, Muncie, Indiana; Dr. Douglass Morse, Brown University, Providence, Rhode Island; and Dr. Simon Pollard, Canterbury Museum, Christchurch, New Zealand, for sharing their expertise and enthusiasm. A special thanks to Skip Jeffery for his support during the creation of this book.

Lerner Publications Company
A division of Lerner Publishing Group, Inc.
241 First Avenue North
Minneapolis, MN 55401 U.S.A.

Website address: www.lernerbooks.com

Library of Congress Cataloging-in-Publication Data

Markle, Sandra.
    Crab spiders : phantom hunters / Sandra Markle.
        p.   cm. — (Arachnid world)
    Includes bibliographical references and index.
    ISBN 978–0–7613–5045–3 (lib. bdg. : alk. paper)
    1. Crab spiders—Juvenile literature. I. Title.
    QL458.4.M347 2012
    595.4'4—dc23   2011020443

Manufactured in the United States of America
1 - DP - 12/31/11

CONTENTS

WELCOME TO THE WORLD OF ARACHNIDS

(ah-RACK-nidz). Arachnids can be found in every habitat on Earth except in the deep ocean.

So how can you tell if an animal is an arachnid rather than a relative like the insect shown below? Both belong to a group of animals called arthropods (AR-throh-podz). All the animals in this group share some traits. They have bodies divided into segments, jointed legs, and a stiff exoskeleton. This is a skeleton on the outside like a suit of armor. One way that usually works to tell if an animal is an arachnid is to count its legs and body parts. While not every adult arachnid has eight legs, most do. Arachnids also usually have two main body parts. Most adult insects, like this dead-leaf-mimic mantis *(right)*, have six legs and three main body parts.

CRAB SPIDER FACT

A crab spider's body temperature rises and falls with the temperature around it. It must warm up to be active.

This book is about crab spiders *(facing page)*. These are arachnids whose body shape and color make them almost disappear, just like some sort of phantom hunter.

CRAB SPIDER

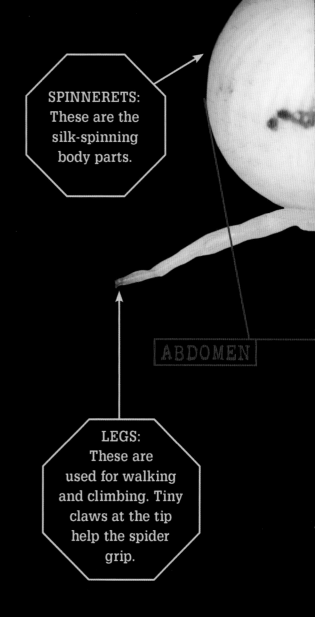

OUTSIDE AND INSIDE

ON THE OUTSIDE

There are about three thousand different kinds of crab spiders. They all have two main body parts: the cephalothorax (sef-uh-loh-THOR-ax) and the abdomen. A tiny waistlike bit called the pedicel joins the two. The spider's exoskeleton is made up of many plates connected by stretchy membranes. This lets the spider bend and move. Take a close look at a female goldenrod crab spider to discover other key features these spiders share.

SPINNERETS: These are the silk-spinning body parts.

ABDOMEN

LEGS: These are used for walking and climbing. Tiny claws at the tip help the spider grip.

PEDICEL

CEPHALOTHORAX

EYES:
These organs detect light and send messages to the brain for sight. Crab spiders usually have eight eyes.

PEDIPALPS:
These are a pair of leglike body parts that extend from the head near the mouth. These help catch and hold prey (living things to eat). In males the pedipalps are also used during reproduction.

CHELICERAE
(keh-LIH-seh-ree): This pair of jawlike parts near the mouth ends in fangs. The fangs are used to stab prey and inject venom (liquid poison).

7

ON THE INSIDE

Look inside an adult female goldenrod crab spider.

BRAIN: This part sends and receives messages to and from other body parts.

PHARYNX (FAR-inks): This muscular tube pumps food into the stomach. Hairs in the tube help filter out solid waste.

VENOM GLAND: This body part produces venom.

TRACHEAE (TRAY-kee-ee): These tubes let air enter through holes called spiracles. Tracheae spread oxygen throughout the spider's body.

COXAL (KAHK-sel) GLANDS: These special groups of cells collect liquid wastes and pass them to the outside of the body.

CAECA (SEE-kuh): These tubes store food.

NERVE GANGLIA: These bundles of nerve tissue send messages between the brain and other body parts.

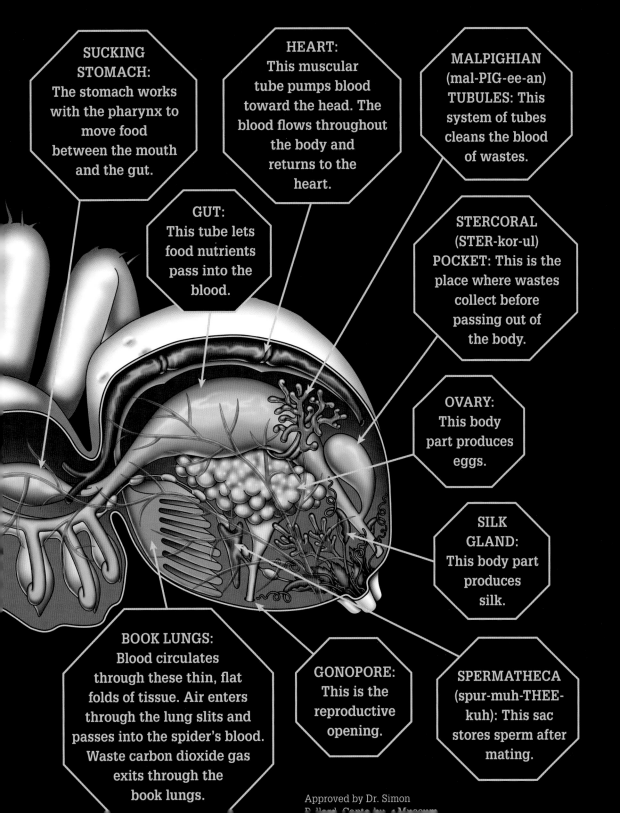

SUCKING STOMACH: The stomach works with the pharynx to move food between the mouth and the gut.

HEART: This muscular tube pumps blood toward the head. The blood flows throughout the body and returns to the heart.

MALPIGHIAN (mal-PIG-ee-an) **TUBULES:** This system of tubes cleans the blood of wastes.

GUT: This tube lets food nutrients pass into the blood.

STERCORAL (STER-kor-ul) **POCKET:** This is the place where wastes collect before passing out of the body.

OVARY: This body part produces eggs.

SILK GLAND: This body part produces silk.

BOOK LUNGS: Blood circulates through these thin, flat folds of tissue. Air enters through the lung slits and passes into the spider's blood. Waste carbon dioxide gas exits through the book lungs.

GONOPORE: This is the reproductive opening.

SPERMATHECA (spur-muh-THEE-kuh): This sac stores sperm after mating.

Approved by Dr. Simon

BECOMING ADULTS

Like all arachnids, crab spiders, such as these Peruvian ant-mimic crab spiders, go through incomplete metamorphosis (meh-tuh-MOHR-fuh-sehs). *Metamorphosis* means "change." A crab spider's life includes three stages: egg, nymph or spiderling, and adult. Crab spiders don't spin silk to catch prey. But they do spin silk to produce a sac around their eggs to protect them. Ant-mimic females build their egg sac *(below)* close to an ant nest. Then they guard their developing young from worker ants. Worker ants will chew their way into the egg sac and eat the eggs.

SOME KINDS OF ARTHROPODS, SUCH AS INSECTS, GO THROUGH COMPLETE METAMORPHOSIS. The four stages are egg, larva, pupa, and adult. Each stage looks and behaves very differently.

Compare the ant-mimic spiderlings to their mother *(below)*. They are smaller, but otherwise, they look much the same. The spiderlings can do most everything adults can do except mate and produce young.

Many spiderlings quickly leave after they hatch. But the ant-mimic spiderlings stay. They are already close to the ants that are their usual prey.

CRAB SPIDER FACT

When this ant-mimic spider catches an ant, it holds it close to its head. This way it looks like two ants communicating instead of like a crab spider eating an ant.

In many kinds of spiders, the males look very similar to the females—just smaller. In most crab spiders, the males and females look very different. Compare the flower spider male to the female. The male is only about half as big as the female, and his body is a different color. Look closely and you'll discover another difference. The female's pedipalps look like little legs. The male's pedipalps look as if they end in boxing gloves. Male crab spiders use their pedipalps to carry their sperm (male reproductive cells). During mating, they insert the sperm into the female's gonopore (reproductive opening).

CRAB SPIDER FACT

Crab spiders
got their name
because they often hold
their front legs extended like
a crab's claws. Sometimes,
they also scurry—crablike—
sideways and backward.

MALE

FEMALE

Whether male or female, spiderlings have to molt (shed their exoskeleton) to grow bigger and to become adults. That's because their exoskeletons don't grow. So as this crab spiderling's body grows bigger, its exoskeleton becomes tight. When it is too tight, the spiderling shoots silk out its spinnerets. The spider uses this silk to anchor itself upside down from a leaf. Its exoskeleton splits open. The spiderling pushes and pulls itself free *(right)*.

The spiderling's body is already covered by a new exoskeleton. The new covering is soft at first. The spiderling's heart pumps blood into its body to make it swell. That stretches the exoskeleton. When the new exoskeleton hardens, the spiderling has room to grow before it has to molt again. The spider will molt between four and seven times to become an adult.

CRAB SPIDER FACT

Spider's silk starts out as a liquid. The spider attaches it to something, even its own leg, and pulls. The liquid becomes a solid silk strand.

OLD EXOSKELETON

LURKING FOR LUNCH

The focus of a crab spider's life is catching insect prey to eat, especially flying insects. Lots of other kinds of spiders also hunt insects. And some kinds of spiders, such as orb weaver spiders, artfully spin silk traps to snag insects out of the air. Crab spiders have developed another way to catch flying insects. They hide where the insects land to eat.

This Australian white crab spider *(right)* hides by climbing into a white flower. The spider stays perfectly still. A silk safety line anchors it in place, and it extends its long front legs.

The flower's nectar (sweet liquid) attracts a honeybee. When the honeybee comes close, the spider snags it with its legs. It uses its legs and its pedipalps to spin the bee around until it's in just the right position. Then the spider sinks its fangs into the bee's body just behind the head. This is a spot where the prey's exoskeleton bends, so it isn't as thick or tough as other body parts. The spider injects deadly venom. The poison lets the spider feed on its prey.

The South American seven-spined crab spider *(below)* doesn't depend on color and shape to hide among flowers. It's just too little to spot easily. A female's body is only about 0.39 inches (10 millimeters) long—about as long as a grain of rice. A male's body is only about half that size.

EYES

The European hairy crab spider *(below)* is even tinier. The bigger females may only be about 0.27 inches (7 mm) long. This spider's covering of long hairs and spikes help it hide and catch plant eaters.

The Costa Rican leaf-mimic crab spider has a built-in disguise. Its body looks like a dead leaf. The spider climbs up a stem. Then by staying still, it hides in full sight to snatch prey. Its disguise also keeps it from being spotted by big, hungry, spider-eating predators (hunters), such as birds or hunting insects.

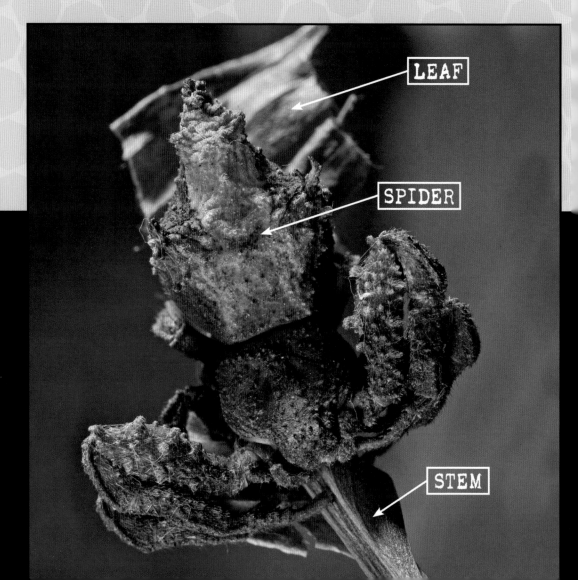

The Madagascar warty bird-dropping crab spider also has a disguise that makes sure it stays safe while it hunts. It looks like a dab of fresh bird waste. Predators pass it by, and prey land right next to it.

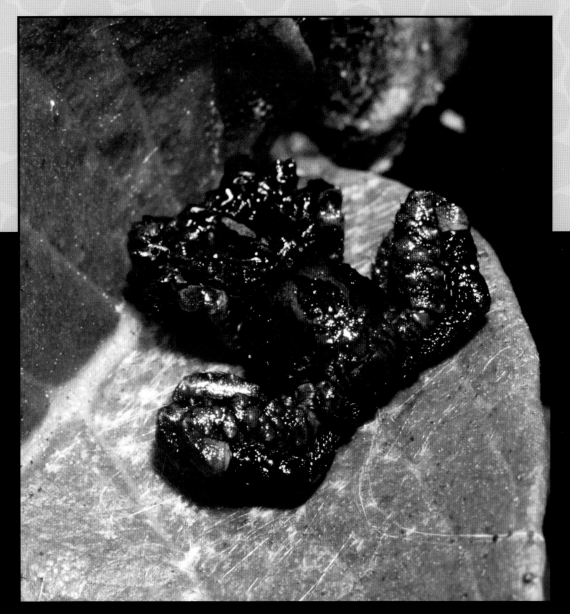

A female North American goldenrod crab spider does something special to help it catch prey. It changes color from yellow to white and back again. With these changes, it is not limited to catching prey only on white flowers or only on yellow flowers.

When a goldenrod crab spider's eyes detect that it is on a yellow background, its body starts making a liquid yellow coloring material. This color flows into the outer cell layer of its body. There it covers the lower layers, which are white. The longer the spider remains on the yellow background, the more yellow color it makes.

The spider becomes completely yellow *(below)* in about a week. It can change from yellow to white much faster—in just a couple of days. That's because it doesn't have to produce more color. The yellow coloring material just flows down to lower layers and passes out of the spider's body with its wastes.

While most crab spiders eat whatever they can snatch, the weaver ant-mimic crab spider mainly eats weaver ants. Its body is perfectly colored and shaped for hunting them. Unlike most crab spiders, the weaver ant-mimic doesn't just sit and wait for prey. It searches out weaver ants and sneaks up on them. Then it runs fast to grab its weaver ant meal.

SPIDER

ANT

The British wandering crab spider also doesn't count on its coloring or a disguise to catch prey. It travels searching for food. When this female saw a fly, it ran fast and lunged. It caught the fly, but another predator—an ant— ran up and attacked the fly too. More ants joined the attack, and the spider lost this prey. It will wander off and keep on hunting.

CRAB SPIDER FACT

When they travel, crab spiders spin a line of silk, called a dragline, behind them. They use sticky silk to anchor this strand to a rock or a branch. If they fall, this silk is their safety line.

ONE SPIDER'S LIFE

It's June in Ohio. The female goldenrod crab spiderling has been hunting since she warmed up this morning. But she missed catching the only fly that came close to her hiding place. Since the day is heating up, she's moving on to search for another hunting spot. She could climb down and walk, but she lifts her rear end and shoots silk from her spinnerets. The breeze catches this silk and gives her a lift.

When she lands, the female spiderling climbs a flower stalk and settles on a bloom. She produces a dab of sticky silk, sticks it to a flower petal, and tugs to create a silk safety line. Then she stays still and waits.

CRAB SPIDER FACT

This spider is called the goldenrod crab spider because it is often seen hunting on flowering goldenrod plants.

Finally, a wasp comes close. The insect is homing in on the scent of nectar. The sensitive hairs all over the female spiderling's body alert her to the air movements stirred by the wasp's wings. When the wasp is very close, the spiderling sees it and tracks it. When the wasp is so close it's almost touching the spiderling, her long front legs swing together. ZAP! She grabs the wasp.

The spiderling bites, injecting paralyzing venom. She bites again. This time she injects digestive juices along with another dose of venom. The digestive juices turn the wasp's soft tissue into a kind of liquid power drink. The muscles around the spider's pharynx and stomach relax to create a sucking force. This force pulls the liquid food out of the prey's exoskeleton and into the spider's body. The spider injects more digestive juices and repeats the process until only the wasp's empty exoskeleton remains. Then the spiderling moves close to the edge of a flower petal and lets this garbage drop.

CRAB SPIDER FACT

The goldenrod crab spider *(right)* is one of the most common kinds of crab spiders. Goldenrod crab spiders live in North America, Europe, and Asia.

A MATE IN WAITING

The female goldenrod crab spiderling continues to travel, hide, and catch prey. When she finds lots of prey in a cluster of yellow flowers, she settles there. Over the following week, her coloring gradually changes from white to yellow. This color change helps hide her from her prey. It also helps her hide from other predators, such as other hunting spiders.

A male goldenrod crab spider has also been attracted to this cluster of flowers. Male spiders molt and become adults as much as three weeks earlier than most females. Like other adult males, this spider is searching for a female of his own kind. When he finds the female goldenrod crab spider, he stays nearby. If another male goldenrod crab spider arrives, he raises his front legs to show his size. Unless the rival is much bigger, he'll even wrestle, trying to bite his opponent.

CRAB SPIDER FACT

If a predator or another male bites a male crab spider on a leg, the bitten spider can snap off the leg at the closest joint (spot that bends) below the body. That keeps the venom from entering the spider's body and killing it.

When the female moves to a nearby plant and another cluster of flowers, the male gives up. Soon another male finds her. The female finally has eaten enough to get the energy she needs to become an adult. She will molt for the last time and mate with the first male of her kind that approaches her.

A nearby male spins a small web. He shifts his abdomen over it and deposits sperm on it. Then he picks up the sperm with a pedipalp. When the female catches a fly and starts to feed, the male climbs onto her abdomen *(right)*. She allows him to stay. He crawls under her and inserts his sperm into her gonopore. After mating, the female crab spider keeps hunting and eating. She needs energy for her eggs to develop. She gets the energy boost she needs by catching bumblebees.

When she is ready to deposit her eggs, she moves away from the flowers where she usually hunts. She settles on a leafy plant. There her eggs are less likely to be attacked by a kind of wasp that seeks out spider egg sacs. This kind of wasp tries to insert one of its own eggs into the spider's egg sac. If the wasp succeeds, the young wasp will grow up eating the spider's developing young.

CRAB SPIDER FACT

An adult
female goldenrod
spider has a body about
0.39 inches (10 mm) long.
The male is only about
0.16 inches (4 mm)
long.

FEMALE

33

The female crab spider spins a silk sheet and lays from seventy-five to three hundred eggs, one at a time. As each egg exits her body, it passes her spermatheca. There each egg joins a sperm and develops a tough coat. The female covers the eggs with more silk. This holds them together and shields them from the weather. The female goldenrod crab spider stays on guard. Inside the egg sac, the baby spiders develop, as they eat their egg's yolk food supply. If any prey or predators come close, the female catches them and eats them. This way she keeps her eggs safe and gains energy.

After about three weeks, the spiderlings hatch. They remain inside the egg sac until they molt once. Next, they chew on the egg sac wall until a hole opens. Then they all escape.

THE CYCLE CONTINUES

Goldenrod crab spider females usually only produce one batch of eggs in a lifetime. Males may try to mate again, but usually they find only one female to mate with.

After leaving the nest, this female goldenrod crab spiderling is on her own. Even her own mother would eat her if she caught her. So the spiderling just naturally knows to hide to escape being spotted by predators. By trial and error, the goldenrod spiderling develops its hunting skills. While it's small, it catches and eats small flies. Each time it molts and grows bigger, it catches bigger flying insects, even honeybees.

Not every spiderling will live to become an adult. Many will become prey for other spiders and insects, such as this assassin beetle *(below)*. Those that live where winters are harsh and hatch from their egg sacs in the autumn won't become adults until the weather warms up again. The autumn weather is soon too cool for the female goldenrod crab spiderling. She crawls down into the leaf litter and curls up inside a rolled, dry leaf. While icy winds blow and snow blankets the ground, she hibernates. That means she's still alive, but all her body processes have slowed down. As a result, she doesn't need to eat. While some crab spiderlings die over the winter, she survives.

When her body warms up in the spring, she crawls out and climbs the stem of a nearby plant. She hides among the flowers that are opening and waits to snatch flies and honeybees. She is a successful hunter and becomes an adult ready to reproduce. A male has already found her and is guarding her. They'll mate. Then she'll catch a bumblebee *(below)*—the largest prey she can catch. With this energy boost, she'll produce eggs. And the crab spider's life cycle will continue.

CRAB SPIDERS AND OTHER DISGUISED ARACHNIDS

CRAB SPIDERS BELONG to a group, or order, of arachnids called Araneae (ah-RAN-ee-eye). These are the spider members of the arachnid group. Crab spiders belong to a family of spiders called the Thomisidae (tom-IHS-ee-dee). There are about three thousand different kinds worldwide.

SCIENTISTS GROUP living and extinct animals with others that are similar. So crab spiders are classified this way:

kingdom: Animalia
phylum: Arthropoda
class: Arachnida
order: Araneae
family: Thomisidae

HELPFUL OR HARMFUL? Crab spiders are mainly helpful because they eat a lot of insects. This helps control insect populations that could otherwise become pests. They also catch and eat lots of honeybees. This isn't helpful for gardeners and honey producers. Crab spiders, like almost all spiders, produce venom to kill their prey. A crab spider's venom is not known to be harmful to people. But some people may have an allergic reaction to any spider's bite.

HOW BIG IS a female goldenrod spider? Its body is about 0.39 inch (10 mm) long.

MORE DISGUISED ARACHNIDS

Crab spiders are arachnids whose body shape and coloring lets them hide and snatch prey. Compare these other skillful hiding spiders.

Ortholasma is a little North American harvestman. Its body is tiny, and its long legs only stretch 0.9 inches (25 mm). It can put on a disguise to stay safe while it hunts for small prey. Its back has ridges that form little pockets. These pockets catch and hold grains of dirt to disguise it. If it senses something big, such as a possible predator, moving nearby, it adds a trick to its disguise. It tightly pulls in its legs, keeps still, and plays dead.

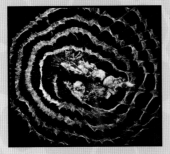

Variable decoy spiders are found in much of Asia, India, and northern Australia. This little spider—females are only 0.4 inches (11 mm) long and males are about half that length—builds an orb web to catch flying prey. It gets its name from the clever way it hides in plain sight on its web. It uses silk to attach a string of garbage down its web. The string may contain the remains of silk-wrapped prey, old egg sacs, and bits of leaves. When the spider climbs onto this line, it hides in plain sight.

Ant-mimic jumping spiders live mainly in warm places in Southeast Asia. They have a body shape that looks like weaver ants. Only about 0.27 inches (7 mm) long, they are even about the same size as the adult ants. These jumping spiders often live in trees close to weaver ant colonies. Because the ants can deliver a severe bite, most predators, such as birds, leave them alone. The spiders are safe to spin a web on a leaf, hide under it, and wait to catch insect prey. Compare this ant-mimic jumping spider to the ant-mimic crab spider on page 24.

GLOSSARY

abdomen: the rear end of an arachnid. It contains systems for digestion, reproduction, and, in spiders, silk production.

adult: the reproductive stage of an arachnid's life cycle

book lungs: thin, flat folds of tissue where blood circulates. Air enters through the lung slits and passes between them, allowing oxygen to enter the blood. Waste carbon dioxide gas is given off through them.

brain: the organ that receives messages from body parts and sends signals to control all body parts

caeca: branching tubes through which liquid food passes and where food is stored. Food nutrients pass from the tubes into the blood and are carried throughout the body.

cephalothorax: the front end of an arachnid. It includes the mouth, the brain, and the eyes. Legs are also attached to this part.

chelicerae: a pair of strong, jawlike parts that extend from the head in front of the mouth and end in fangs that inject venom

coxal glands: special groups of cells for collecting and getting rid of liquid wastes through openings to the outside of the body. They aid in maintaining water balance in the body.

egg: a female reproductive cell; also the name given to the first stage of an arachnid's life cycle

exoskeleton: a protective, armorlike covering on the outside of the body

eyes: sensory organs that detect light and send signals to the brain for sight

fang: one of a pair of toothlike parts of the spider's chelicerae. Venom flows out of the fang through a hole near the tip.

gut: a body part through which food nutrients pass into the blood and are carried throughout the body

heart: the muscular tube that pumps blood throughout the body

Malpighian tubules: a system of tubes that cleans the blood of wastes and dumps them into the gut

molt: the process of an arachnid shedding its exoskeleton

nerve ganglia: bundles of nerve tissue that send messages between the brain and other body parts

ovary: the body part that produces eggs

pedicel: the waistlike part in spiders that connects the cephalothorax to the abdomen

pedipalps: a pair of leglike body parts that extend from the head near the mouth. These help catch prey and hold it for eating. In males the pedipalps are also used during reproduction.

pharynx: a muscular body part that contracts to create a pumping force, drawing food into the body's digestive system. Hairs filter out hard waste bits.

silk gland: the body part that produces silk

sperm: a male reproductive cell

spermatheca: a sac in female arachnids that stores sperm after mating

spiderling: the name given to the stage between egg and adult in spiders

spinneret: the body part that spins silk

spiracle: a small opening in the exoskeleton that leads into the trachea

stercoral pocket: a place where body wastes collect before passing out of the body

sucking stomach: the muscular stomach that, along with the pharynx, pulls liquid food into the arachnid's gut. Cells in the lining produce digestive juices.

tracheae: tubes that help spread oxygen that enters through holes, called spiracles, throughout the spider's body

venom: liquid poison

venom gland: the body part that produces venom

DIGGING DEEPER

To keep on investigating crab spiders, explore these books and online sites.

BOOKS

Bishop, Nic. *Nic Bishop Spiders*. New York: Scholastic, 2007. Fantastic, real-life photos and text let you compare crab spiders to other kinds of spiders.

Singer, Marilyn. *Venom*. Minneapolis: Milllbrook Press, 2007. Find out about creatures that can hurt or even kill with a bite or a sting.

Wheeler, Jill. *Crab Spiders*. Edina, MN: Checkerboard Books, 2005. Learn even more about the traits and behavior of crab spiders.

MORE FROM SANDRA MARKLE

ARACHNID WORLD:

Black Widows

Harvestmen

Orb Weavers

Scorpions

Ticks

Wolf Spiders

WEBSITES

Crab Spiders

http://www.crabspider.org/videos

Discover lots of videos and photos of crab spiders in action.

The Garden Safari

http://www.gardensafari.net/english/garden_spiders.htm

Visit a photographer's garden. Discover the crab spiders living there. Explore what other spiders share this garden home.

LERNER e SOURCE™

Visit www.lernerresource.com for free, downloadable arachnid diagrams, research assignments to use with this series, and additional information about arachnid scientific names.

CRAB SPIDER ACTIVITY

To get a feel for how crab spiders hunt, try this. Pick one spot in a room and put on clothes that will hide you in plain sight in that spot. Tie a 1-yard-long (0.9-meter) piece of string to the middle of a tissue. Next, sit on a chair in your hiding spot stretching your arms out ready to grab. Have a partner stand behind you and dangle the tissue in front of you. Instruct your partner to yank the tissue away quickly when you move. Like a crab spider snatching a flying insect, you'll have to be quick to catch your prey. Repeat this five times. How many times did you catch your prey?

INDEX

PHOTO ACKNOWLEDGMENTS

The images in this book are used with the permission of: © Michael & Patricia Fogden/CORBIS, p. 4; © Kim Taylor/naturepl.com, pp. 5, 39; © iStockphoto.com/Henrik Larsson, pp. 6–7; © Laura Westlund/Independent Picture Service, pp. 8–9; © Joe Warfel/Eighth-Eye Photography, pp. 10, 11, 18 (inset), 31; © Stephen Dalton/naturepl.com, p. 13; © David Kuhn, p. 15; © Ed Nieuwenhuys, pp. 16–17, 22, 23; © Premaphotos/naturepl.com, pp. 18, 21, 25, 32–33, 41 (center); © Emanuele Biggi/Tips RM/Glow Images, p. 19; © Minden Pictures/SuperStock, pp. 20, 41 (bottom); © Premaphotos/Alamy, p. 24; © David Wrobel/Visuals Unlimited, Inc., pp. 26–27, 29; © All Canada Photos/SuperStock, pp. 30, 36–37; © Paul Zahl/National Geographic/Getty Images, pp. 34–35; © Anthony Bannister; Gallo Images/CORBIS, p. 38; © Marshal Hedin, p. 41 (top); © Simon Pollard, pp. 46–47.

Front cover: © Ray Coleman/Visuals Unlimited, Inc.

Main body text set in Glypha LT Std 55 Roman 12/20. Typeface provided by Adobe Systems.